The Linden Tree

Mary Gavin

The Heart of the Linden

The Linden Tree is an ancient tree. It can live up to, and beyond, 2,000 years old. It was known as 'The Tree of Peace' whose tonics and teas could cure anxiety and tension. It is a resilient tree with heart shaped leaves and fragrant blossom loved by bees.

A sign of resilience, rebirth and renewal in each person, in Community and eventually the World.

May the Linden tree, celebrated since the dawn of time, bring you calm and rejuvenation in these turbulent times...

If...

If you find this book it must be because I made this book for you. It is said that all things happen for a reason...

Ultimately we have just one moral duty: to reclaim large areas of peace in ourselves, more and more peace, and to reflect it towards others. And the more peace there is in us, the more peace there will be in our troubled world.

Etty Hillesum (1914-1943)

Poems 1993—2023

11	The Moment
13	A Song
15	Simply
17	An Ordinary Woman
19	Timeless Linden
21	A Bird
23	The Dust
25	Anxious Eyes
27	Imagine
29	The Ground
31	The Pause
33	Earth's Cradle
35	Home
37	Every Poem
39	The Portrait's Eyes
41	The Writing Box
43	A Single Candle
45	The Artist
47	About the Author
49	Acknowledgements

The Moment

Stillness, hush…
Nowhere to go.

Meet the moment
Silence, rest, deep connection.

Stillness, hush…
Palpable presence.

Connection
Together enfolded

In Loving
Presence…

The Moment.

A Song

In the depths
Of my being
A song arose
A song of Peace.

A song for me
A song 'maybe'
For you
Too.

Singing
Of the Miracle
That is
Me

That is
You
That is
All…

Just as
It is.
This is
Simplicity.

Simply...

Simply
A new way of being...
There is nothing
To achieve.

No Important
Position to maintain
No big house
To buy.

All you need
To do
Is be
Who you are...

Do what
You are doing
And extend
Your heart...

An Ordinary Woman

To look at her
You wouldn't think it
She would pass
you by
And you
Wouldn't glance.

Yet...
Her life
She has lived it
With courage
And grace
And taking her chance.

Some days
Her stomach churns
With fear
of memories past
Still etched
Upon her face

Yet...
Her lips and eyes
They smile
She carries
Herself
With such grace.

I see them
Every day
They move in
And out of my world
A flickering second
And then it's gone
The public face
Is back again.

Timeless Linden

The Linden Tree
Calms my heartbeat...
It stands still
Deeply rooted
Whilst change
Surrounds it.

It stays
Constant
It just is...
And the birds
Make it
Their home.

A Bird

To be...
a bird
hovering...
being supported
on a stream
of air
and
watching...
watching
the water
flow
the refugees
flow
To see...
blocks of
ice
melting,
melding
with
nature's
flow
so
gently
so
tenderly.

And this
I learnt
from
being
a bird.

The Dust

The dust
Is just the World
It is not you
You know...

Who are you?

You are beautiful
You are original
You are Creation
itself.

Anxious Eyes

Anxiety flickers on anxious faces
Shaking energy
In shaking bodies
Reflecting chaotic times we live in…

Where are our strong roots?
Our roots to nature
Our roots to the earth
To people, animals and plants?

Why have we created
A reality in which
It is not safe to love
To be vulnerable

To be human…
So we mask
What is real
And 'perform' what is not

Yet… our eyes speak what is real
Our bodies demonstrate the truth
Why?
Why can we not just be us?

Maybe... we can...
If... we listen deeply to
The gifts
Each moment, each day sends

Imagine

Imagine…
A new reality
Being born
In which…

We will look deeper
And see
That all
Is part of Creation.

A time of rebirth
Of kindness
Of understanding
Of patience.

A realisation
That everything
All
Is part of the Mystery unfolding…

The World itself
A miraculous
Symphony
Of beauty

In many
Forms.

The Ground

The ground
Of my being
Is silent
Is still...
Quieten
Your mind
Still your being
Let the swirling water
That is you
Settle...
Into
Your true home
Peace.

The Pause

It happens often
within the pause

my essence whispers
peace...

a tingling sound
a gentle breeze

a loss of time
of space, of place

within that gap
such beauty found

when love, she whispers peace

Earth's Cradle

water
cradles
the
light

light
cradles
the
water

Home

Between
The sky
And the earth
I listen
To the whispers…
And gently
Build my
Home.

Every poem

It is said
That beyond...
Faith
There are
No words
But words
Evolve
As we
Evolve
Deep...
Experience
Reach and
Find words
Or create words
Anew...
Words
As bridges,
As sparks
Of light
As music
As sound ciphers
Between
Here and there
Like
Swirling tunnels
Of connection
Of creativity
Of poetry.

It is said
That every poem
Was once a word
How then can words
Not exist
Beyond...?

Well
Maybe
Their seeds do.

The Portrait's Eyes

The portrait is old now
The surface creased
The eyes are sharp though
Their light intense.

They tell a story
For those who 'see'
Of challenge, of life
Of love, of strength.

They whisper in silence
For those who 'hear'
BE passion, BE love
BE wild, BE free.

Across the time
But in this space
It's the eyes, they say
to me
BE free...

Inspired by the portrait of Charlotte Bronte in the sitting room of 84 Plymouth Grove, Manchester. The home of Elizabeth Gaskell

The Writing Box

The sounds of that time
Resonate in this silent space still now
This precious moment
Infused with that precious past.

Past, present, future
Merge in the audible and tangible atmosphere
As the quill in the writing box
Rushes to record the moment.

Be still...
Listen...
To the haunting sound
Of a genius at work.

Dedicated to Women writers throughout history who wrote their way to peace but were mostly ignored.

A Single Candle

A darkened room
A single candle
Lit...
A gentle light
Everywhere.

The Artist

She's wild and free
An artist...
Painting her life afresh each day
With words.

She passes through
And leaves
Silent as a breeze
Leaving others richer.

Like a forest scattered with
Freshly fallen leaves
Like the ground's thirst
Watered by droplets

From a fountain...

About the author

Mary taught for twenty-four years. She specialised in health education, Eco and Peace education. She always loved the writing process and the teaching of writing.

Poetry is the main way her mind interacts with the world – in images, rhythms, sound and light. She loves to translate her experience into as few words as possible and make those experiences accessible to her readers. She loves photography for the same reason.

Her first poetry book 'Blossoms of the Heart' has been translated this year into Japanese and five poems have featured each season in Coal Sack magazine (Tokyo) in both English and Japanese. Mary's poetry also featured in 'The Meeting'- A book inspired by John Clare to celebrate two hundred years since his first poetry book was published. Published by the John Clare Society. Her writing connected with peace education has featured in the Portico Quarterly and also in the work of Peaceful Schools UK.

This is her second poetry collection.

August 2024

Acknowledgements

I wish to thank Alex Lewis and Daniel Dobson at Smallprint Studio, without whose technological expertise this poetry book would not exist. Also to the landscape which inspired many of these words.

All text and content © Mary Gavin 2024
Designed and published by Smallprint Studio
ISBN 978-0-9934686-3-6